God Is . . .

God Is . . .

A 10-Week Interactive Devotional

By Victoria White

Unless otherwise noted, all Scripture quotations are taken from THE HOLY BIBLE, NEW INTERNATIONAL VERSION®, NIV® Copyright © 1973, 1978, 1984, 2011 by Biblica, Inc.® Used by permission. All rights reserved worldwide. Scripture quotations marked AMP are taken from the Amplified® Bible, copyright © 2015 by The Lockman Foundation. Used by permission. (www.Lockman.org). Scripture quotations marked CSB are taken from the Christian Standard Bible®, Copyright © 2017 by Holman Bible Publishers. Used by permission. Christian Standard Bible® and CSB® are federally registered trademarks of Holman Bible Publishers. Scripture quotations marked ESV are taken from the ESV® Bible (The Holy Bible, English Standard Version®), copyright © 2001 by Crossway, a publishing ministry of Good News Publishers. Used by permission. All rights reserved. Scripture quotations marked KJV are taken from the King James Version of the Bible. (Public Domain.) Scripture quotations marked NASB are taken from the New American Standard Bible®, copyright © 1960, 1995 by The Lockman Foundation. Used by permission. (www.Lockman.org). Scripture quotations marked NLT are taken from the Holy Bible, New Living Translation, copyright © 1996, 2007 by Tyndale House Foundation. Used by permission of Tyndale House Publishers, Inc., Carol Stream, Illinois 60188. All rights reserved.

This book is dedicated to my parents.

Most everything I do is for you both, but especially this work. In life and in death, you led me to closeness and encounter with Christ. Your labor was tremendous; enjoy your rest and your reward.

- Victoria

Table of Contents

Week 1 1

Week 2 11

Week 3 20

Week 4 29

Week 5 39

Week 6 49

Week 7 59

Week 8 69

Week 9 79

Week 10 89

Notes 100

Answer Key 102

Acknowledgements 104

A Word from the Author

This project was no easy task. First, I've never considered myself a writer. I do a much better job explaining my thoughts and feelings through conversation and verbal storytelling than I do on paper. For that reason, I decided to just be me and make this devotional (devo) a conversation. At certain points on the writing journey, I pictured myself having the conversation with specific people in my life – a coworker, my neighbor Nora, even some of the students I lead at Sam Houston State University. Honestly, I wanted my writing to sound like me talking to you as if we were sitting down to coffee and good conversation.

God Is . . . is simply me sharing my stories and thoughts. I often say, "The gospel is not just a story to be told; it is a truth to be experienced." That's what *God Is . . .* sharing my experiences and encounters with Christ in the hope that they give you an opportunity to encounter the gospel and know Jesus personally.

Another goal I have is to encourage you to think outside the box when it comes to how you spend time with God each day. At one point, I felt like my devotional time was becoming too routine and structured, and I needed something new. This challenged me to think about devo time outside of just reading the Bible, taking notes, praying, and listening. I began to meditate on Scripture, journal past experiences, write out my prayers, listen to Christian music, and even read gospel-centered books. This allowed me to look for God, to listen for God in places and spaces I had never looked or listened before. It grew me so much that I decided to structure *God Is* . . . in this way, hoping to give you an opportunity to try it as well. As you go through this devotional, each day will allow you to spend time with God in a unique way.

If you attend church every Sunday, I recommend starting each week (Day 1) on Monday. This will be great for the way each Day 7 is set up.

Before You Begin

Each seven-day week consists of a daily devotional reading and activity centered around a characteristic or attribute of God: who He's proven Himself to be. The intent is to learn who God is in our lives.

Day 1: I introduce a scripture from the Bible and couple it with some simple and practical teaching. Consider this my novice commentary and initial thoughts on the text.

Day 2: I share my personal experience with God concerning the attribute for that week. I want to invite you into my personal journey with Christ—the good, the bad, the messy, and the growth!

Day 3: This is a day for prayer! Read through the prayer I've written for that day, and then use the space provided to journal your own prayer.

Day 4: I provide a #QOTD (quote of the day) and a #SOTD (song of the day). This will encourage gospel-centered reading, and it'll revolutionize your playlist. If you're not a music buff like me, feel free to just read over the lyrics of the song to provoke further thought.

Day 5: This is a day of guided journaling and reflection. It may include prompts, questions, or just some thought-provoking sentiments for you to ponder and then journal about. I know there's lots of journaling; the intent is to create an opportunity for you to document your journey with Christ.

Day 6: You get a *Who Am I?* quiz about a Bible character. There is only *one* answer, but I give you three clues. Shout out if you guess correctly after clue number one! Be sure to check your answer by using the Answer Key at the back of the book. Feel free to read through the scripture references listed there as well.

Day 7: Today is called Selah. *Selah* is a word that encourages you to pause the busyness of life and consider and reflect over the lessons from the week. Since this devo is meant to be interactive, I have created space for you to journal any thoughts you want to remember.

Alright, let's learn and grow together!

Week 1: God Is . . . Always Good

Day 1

Taste and see that the LORD is good. Oh, the joys of those who take refuge in him!

Psalm 34:8 (NLT)

In dark and dreary seasons of life, one lie the Enemy often tells us is that God is some fickle, wishy-washy god whom we need to catch on a "good day," or that we need to work harder for and be better if we want to receive goodness from Him.

Don't believe that lie. God is *always good*! Goodness is His irreversible nature, and no occurrence, no circumstance, no storm is powerful enough to change the character of our good God.

Satan, the Father of Lies, would have you believe that God's identity is determined by how you feel. However, the truth is, your emotions are fickle, not God. He is consistent and steady. "Jesus Christ is the same yesterday, today, and forever" (Hebrews 13:8). Once God reveals a part of His character to you, be assured that it's who He has been all along and who He will always be. If He has ever been good, He must still be good, and He will always be good. It's His nature to be good to us.

God Is . . . ALWAYS GOOD

When we don't deserve it, when we don't appreciate it, when we fail to recognize it, and especially when we don't feel like it, God Is *always good*.

Now, taste and see, take the risk, try God, and at every juncture of life, you will find Him being who He is: *good*.

God Is . . . ALWAYS GOOD

Day 2

This truth, that God is *always good*, has become the foundation of my relationship with Him. There was a time in my life when I believed God was good, but when trouble came, when life *really* started happening, I attributed characteristics to Him that He couldn't possibly possess. I did this because I had no understanding that He never ceases to be good.

For years while my dad battle sickness, I begged God to spare his life because I couldn't imagine living without him. My mother had passed away many years before and the thought of having to endure that kind of pain a second time seemed unbearable. I pleaded with God to just be *good* to me and my family this go-around.

The Lord began to teach me the truth about His nature. He reminded me of all the times in my life that He had proven His goodness to me. I told Him that I would remain rooted in the truth that goodness cannot be separated from God.

On April 1, 2016, I gathered with my sisters and brothers-in-law around my dad's hospital bed. My oldest sister was reading Scripture as the monitor that had been quietly beeping in the background started making the sound we were all dreading: the sustained tone of death. It seemed to be one of the longest moments of my life; seconds stretched into minutes as we stood by our father, watching life leave his body. As I grabbed my dad's hand, the tremble traveled from my hand to my voice, but with every ounce of strength I could muster, I began to sing, "Lord You are good, good, oh, oh. Yes, You are good, you're good oh, oh." God's presence invaded the room and blanketed us that morning. I was hurting, and I was sad, but I was certain that God was still good!

God Is . . . ALWAYS GOOD

Day 3

Today, pray the prayer below and give glory to God for His unending goodness.

God, without petition or request, I come to You today to simply thank You for Your goodness in my life. Thank You for this week's reminder that in all things, at all times, You are good. No more believing the devil's lies. You are *always good*! Even in the dark days of life, I will search for Your goodness in full confidence that I will find it. Just like David, I will not fear when I walk through dim valleys because You are with me. I am convinced that Your goodness and Your mercy will follow me every day of my life. I will walk with confident belief in Your promises. You are my God, and You are always good. My prayer today is that I hold tight to this truth. It is in the matchless name of Jesus Christ I pray.

Amen.

At some point today, continue this exercise on the next page by journaling your own prayer of thanksgiving to God for always being good.

God Is . . . ALWAYS GOOD

Prayer Journal

_____
_____
_____
_____
_____
_____
_____
_____
_____
_____
_____
_____
_____
_____
_____

God Is . . . ALWAYS GOOD

Day 4

Today's #QOTD is from Craig Groeschel, author of *The Christian Atheist: Believing in God but Living as If He Doesn't Exist*.

"If God has done what you think he should do, trust him. If God doesn't do what you think he should do, trust him. If you pray and believe God for a miracle and he does it, trust Him. If your worst nightmare comes true, believe he is sovereign. Believe he is good."[1]

Today's #SOTD is "King of My Heart" by Bethel Music. Of course, use this space to journal your thoughts, feelings, and reflections after reading this quote and hearing this song.

_____
_____
_____
_____
_____
_____
_____
_____
_____
_____

God Is . . . ALWAYS GOOD

Day 5

Today is a day of reflection. Use the space below to record some of the times in your life when you have experienced the goodness of God. Some of them might be obvious to you, but challenge yourself to recall the times that you almost missed His goodness because of the difficulties you were facing.

_____
_____
_____
_____
_____
_____
_____
_____
_____
_____
_____
_____
_____
_____
_____
_____
_____

God Is . . . ALWAYS GOOD

Day 6

Clue 1:

I was a wealthy man who lived a great life with my large family and even larger flocks. I loved and served the Lord and I aimed to please Him in all that I did.

Clue 2:

As the devil was looking for someone to attack, God mentioned my name as a good consideration because He knew that I was confident in His goodness in all things.

Clue 3:

I lost all of my flocks, my servants, and my children in different catastrophes. I experienced extreme physical illness, lost the support of my closest friends and even my wife. I mourned, I was sad, but I resolved to trust God and refrain from evil. I acknowledged God's unlimited power and admitted my human weaknesses. God restored my health and my flocks, increased my family, and gave me a long life in Him.

Who am I? _____

God Is . . . ALWAYS GOOD

Day 7

Selah

Have you allowed your feelings to attribute characteristics to God that don't truly belong to Him? I encourage you to dispel those lies. Study God's Word, spend time with Him in prayer, recall your history with Him, and get to know Him as a Father who is always good. I encourage you to be intentional in spending time being mindful of this truth today.

_____
_____
_____
_____
_____
_____
_____
_____
_____
_____
_____
_____
_____

Week 2: God Is . . . NEAR

Day 1

*The L*ORD *is near to the brokenhearted and saves the crushed in spirit.*

Psalm 34:18 (ESV)

Have you ever had a broken heart? Do you remember how lonely you felt? How isolated you *desired* to be? Even when friends and family members tried to be present and show their love and support, your brokenness caused you to push them away. I believe we often do this same thing with God, who desires to be near us.

Because of how we feel, we allow our busy schedules, our broken hearts, and even our burdened spirits to push God away. But remember, our feelings don't change the nature of Almighty God, and it's His nature to be close to us. The word *"near"* in Psalm 34:18 comes from the Hebrew word *karov*. It literally means that God is close enough to touch. When we believe this truth of who God is, He doesn't seem like some huge God beyond the sky who sits and watches us endure life's trials; rather, He becomes the God who walks closely through every stage of life with us. He becomes a near God! It's in Genesis 3 when Adam disobeyed God's command by eating the fruit of the Tree of the Knowledge of Good and Evil.

God Is . . . NEAR

After he sinned against God, Adam responded like many of us would—he hid, thinking, *I cannot be seen by a holy God when I'm in this condition.* Does that sound familiar to you at all?

Satan sends feelings of guilt and regret, shame and condemnation to try to force us outside of God's presence. But just as He did for Adam, God is walking through the garden, searching for us. He's calling out to us because He desires closeness with each of us. He knows where we have fallen short, and He is aware that life's circumstances have caused us to lose faith in Him. He knows and still He's calling us to closeness because that's just who God is. He sent His Son to die to gain closeness with us. Not just so that we can spend eternity with Him when we die, but so that even on earth, we can live relationally with Him, inviting Him to be part of our everyday lives. We can give Him permission to engage and interact with us through others and to speak sweetly to us in moments when the Enemy would have us believe He's abandoned us.

God is near. When we don't feel Him, He's near. When life's happenings seem cruel and we can't understand why God would allow us to experience such hurt, He's near. When we fall victim to our own fleshly desires rather than commanding our flesh to submit to the authority of Christ, He's still near.

God Is . . . NEAR
Day 2

I felt most secluded from God back in 2005 when my mother passed away. Because I did not truly understand the nature of God or the truth that He is always good, I felt as if God had lied to me. I vividly remember my "conversation" with Him the day she passed: "You said you were a healer. Why didn't You heal her? If You're all powerful, why didn't You display Your power and perform the miracle that we prayed for? Why did You leave my family here to deal with this?"

God, in His gracious nature, allowed me to feel how I felt, say what I needed to say, and then, through His Word, He lovingly answered me. "I will never leave you or forsake you. I am with you always, even until the end of the age. Even when you walk through the valley of the shadow of death, you don't have to be afraid because I am with you." It was during that time, I learned that God is not intimidated by our honesty, and He can handle the truth of our hearts. When you pray to God honestly, He reveals Himself to you, and He proves to you who He has always been.

God stayed right there with me and called out to me in hopes that I would allow Him to be as close as He desired to be. I had to choose to trust God. I'm human, so some days were easier to choose that truth than others. Some days I gave it my all, and I failed. He extended His grace toward me until one day I chose to walk in closeness with Him and to believe that He is always near. My life has never been the same!

God Is . . . NEAR
Day 3

Today, pray the prayer below and thank God for always being near.

Father, You are near! I will declare this truth when I feel You, and even when I don't. I pray that I am always rooted in the truth of Your Word that promises You won't ever leave me or forsake me. I pray that You teach me to depend on Your closeness in times of trouble. Teach me to look for You when I don't feel You, to turn to You when I need You, and to always rest in Your presence. I place my confidence in You today. I choose to live relationally with You, involving You in every aspect of my day. You are real, You live inside of me, and Your love flows through me. You don't desire just to use me to impact others, but You desire to be near me and do life with me! My prayer today is that I hold tight to this truth. It is in the powerful name of Jesus Christ I pray.

Amen.

Also, at some point today, continue this exercise on the next page by journaling your own prayer of how your life is made better because of His closeness.

God Is . . . NEAR

Prayer Journal

_____
_____
_____
_____
_____
_____
_____
_____
_____
_____
_____
_____
_____
_____
_____
_____
_____

God Is . . . NEAR

Day 4

Today's #QOTD is from Meister Eckhart.

"I am as sure as I live that nothing is so near to me as God. God is nearer to me than I am to myself; my existence depends on the nearness and the presence of God."[2]

Today's #SOTD is "Abba" by Jonathan David Helser. Of course, use this space to journal your thoughts, feelings, and reflections after reading this quote and hearing this song

_____

_____

_____

_____

_____

_____

_____

_____

_____

_____

_____

_____

God Is . . . NEAR

Day 5

Today is a day of reflection. Use the space below to record some of the times in your life when you recall God's nearness. Some of them might be obvious, but challenge yourself to think of those times when you felt abandoned by God but now, in retrospect, realize He was with you all along.

_____
_____
_____
_____
_____
_____
_____
_____
_____
_____
_____
_____
_____
_____
_____
_____
_____
_____
_____
_____

God Is . . . NEAR

Day 6

Clue 1:

I was a disciple of Jesus. I followed both Him and his teachings during His time on earth.

Clue 2:

I learned that being a disciple of Jesus doesn't automatically make you a faith giant because I wrestled with the truth that Jesus had risen from the dead.

Clue 3:

I recognize that my doubt was a human weakness. Because of God's grace to me, in my moment of doubt, Jesus came near to me and appeared again just for me.

Who am I? _____

God Is . . . NEAR

Day 7

Selah

Have you allowed God to be as close as He desires to be to you? If not, go back and find the place where you first doubted His nearness. Just like He did for Thomas in John chapter 20, He will reveal himself and show you just how near He always is. Look back and see how He kept you. Find His hands holding you together. Now be assured moving forward that *this* is who God is. I encourage you to spend some intentional time being mindful of this truth today.

_____
_____
_____
_____
_____
_____
_____
_____
_____
_____
_____
_____
_____

Week 3: God Is . . . Constant

Day 1

But You, O LORD, abide forever, And Your name to all generations.

Psalm 102:12 (NASB)

Due to the closeness in meaning and the many similarities, the words *consistent* and *constant* are used interchangeably. In many uses, this may be acceptable; however, I believe there is a noteworthy difference we must acknowledge when talking about the nature and character of God. While it is true that God is consistent, to say that He is constant tries to apply a new meaning that the word *consistent* does not encompass. Let's quickly look at these differences from a natural perspective.

We who are employed are *consistently* paid for the work we do, usually once a week, bi-weekly, or monthly. You can always count on payday because it is consistent! Now, it would be a blessing to the infinite power if our salaries were *constantly* placed in our accounts. Day in and day out, moment after moment, around the clock our check are repeatedly and perpetually being deposited into our accounts. *That* would be constant! *Consistent* indicates an expected and anticipated behavior or action over a period of time, but *constant* suggests that there is no expectation of change or end.

God Is . . . Constant
Day 2

I was preparing to expound on the times in my life when God was constant, and then I realized that it is impossible to do that! I would be writing a story that begins at the genesis of time that continues without the possibility of ending. I thought of the old "church mothers" I grew up with and hearing them testify, "He kept me from dangers seen and *unseen*. He kept my enemies away." I considered how often I lived carefree, with no real concept or understanding that God's being constant was the only thing preventing calamity, present threat or danger, and even the fulfillment of the plans of my enemies. That's a story far too long to tell, so I figured I'd just continue with my thoughts from yesterday.

Many times we think of God as consistent. We can look back over our lives and see His track record of how He always came through each time we needed Him. Even if He didn't come when we wanted or expected, as my momma would say, He was always right on time. What if I told you that God must be far better than consistent because even HR departments are typically consistent? Because He is God, the one true and living God, He must be something that no one else is capable of being: *constant*.

Our understanding of who God is will increase when we grasp this concept that His character is constant. Not only did He heal you when you were sick, but each morning you wake up without illness, it's because He's constantly warding off the Enemy. He doesn't sit in heaven like Clark Kent at his desk until you find yourself in crisis, and then He heads to His heavenly telephone booth to become your Superman. That would be consistent. But consider the great majority of the crises that the Enemy designed for your life never touched you because He's not Superman, He is God. He does not need a telephone booth to become what He never ceased being. God is not His costume; being God is not what He does. God is His nature, and God is who He constantly is. He intercedes for us (Romans 8:34); He goes before us to defeat our enemies (Deuteronomy 1:30); He is immutable and prevents us from being consumed (Malachi 3:6). He never stops moving; He never stops giving; He never stops pursuing. When we don't see it, when we don't know it, when we don't feel it, He is working and He is God. He is *constant*!

God Is . . . Constant
Day 3

Today, pray the prayer below and thank God for being what we often fail to realize—constant.

Lord, today I stop and recognize that You just never stop being! You are God and You are constant! I'm thankful that You step in when I need you, when I call You, when I expect You. But today, I pause to thank You for never leaving me and never ceasing to be even when I have no clue that You are being. I'm so grateful that You aren't fickle like humans; You don't need advanced notice, You don't have to prepare, and You don't wait for an invitation into the happenings of your children's lives, You just are. You are there; You are present; You are moving and working and doing and being. You are constant! Thank You for Your faithfulness. Forgive me for each time I have failed to recognize how You were keeping me. I ask that You help me to be aware of Your presence and assured of Your nature. My prayer today is that I hold tight to the truth that You are CONSTANT. It is in the majestic name of Jesus Christ I pray.

Amen.

At some point today, continue this exercise on the next page by journaling your own prayer of how your life is made better because He never stops being who He is.

God Is . . . Constant

Prayer Journal

God Is . . . Constant

Day 4

Today's #QOTD is from Jack Wellman.

"If there was anything we could say about God it is that He is steadfast and that He is the steadfast anchor of our soul. . . . We have no steadfastness outside of our faith in Christ."[3]

Today's #SOID is "Constant One" by Steffany Gretzinger. Of course, use this space to journal your thoughts, feelings, and reflections after reading this quote and hearing this song.

_____
_____
_____
_____
_____
_____
_____
_____
_____
_____
_____
_____

God Is . . . Constant

Day 5

Today is a day of reflection. Use the space below to record some of the times in your life when you failed to realize at the moment, but now you see, that the constant grace of God was the only thing that kept you. You may describe a good time in your life, even a perfect day. This may be a time when you didn't recognize the Enemy was after you. But thinking about it now, you know that the Enemy never takes a break from this battle. There, in that realization, lies the proof that God was there, constantly fighting for you.

_____

_____

_____

_____

_____

_____

_____

_____

_____

_____

_____

_____

_____

God Is . . . Constant

Day 6

Clue 1:

I was not a well-liked sibling by my eleven brothers and one sister. I'm not talking about your average sibling rivalry.

Clue 2:

I once told my siblings about a dream. Out of jealousy and anger, they threw me into a pit and sold me into slavery. Slave traders took me into Egypt and sold me to Potiphar. I was unaware at the time, but God was at work in my life, even then.

Clue 3:

It's a long story, but from Potiphar's house I ended up in prison. I became friends with the prison keeper when he learned of my ability to interpret dreams. Although I was locked away in prison, God was constant behind the scenes. At the appropriate time, God revealed how He was orchestrating my life. He brought the dream I had shared with my brothers to reality and put me in a place of greatness allowing me to save my adopted nation from starvation.

Who am I? _____

God Is . . . Constant

Day 7

Selah

Have you ever failed to realize that God is constant? How many new ways can you find to thank Him with this revelation? Take a moment to thank God for things you never recognized as a part of His constant nature. Appreciate Him for His never-ending, never-changing nature. I encourage you to be intentional in spending time being mindful of this truth today.

_____

_____

_____

_____

_____

_____

_____

_____

_____

_____

_____

_____

_____

Week 4: God Is . . . LOVE

Day 1

But God proves his own love for us in that while we were still sinners, Christ died for us.

Romans 5:8 (CSB)

But anyone who does not love does not know God, for God is love.

1 John 4:8 (NLT)

If you've been a part of the Christian faith for any amount of time, I'm sure you've heard this truth over and over and over again: God is love. Truth be told, as many times as we have heard it, the great majority of believers still don't comprehend this truth. Love is not just what God gives us and requires of us, both toward Him and others, but love is who God is.

Merriam-Webster's Dictionary defines love as "strong affection for another arising out of kinship or personal ties." A second definition states that love is "affection based on admiration, benevolence, or common interests." The phrases that leaped from the pages as I read these definitions were "arising out of" and "based on." These words imply that this love is conditional, that it requires something in exchange. This is generally how humans love; we offer love to someone based on their fulfillment of some requirement or stipulation we have put in place. This conditional love that is rooted in fickle and fleeting emotions and feelings is not at all a reflection of the love that God embodies and provides.

When God proved His love for us by sending His only begotten Son to die for our sin, He had no reason to love us. That's the reality of who God is. He needs no reason to love us because love is who He is. His nature is the sole justification for His behavior!

We must be careful not to misinterpret the verse in 1 John, which tells us that God is love; this does not have the same meaning as God is a loving God. Love, in this text, is not a meager attribute, but it is the very nature and essence of God. Love finds its origin in God, and the two never existed apart from the other.

I'm kind of leaving you hanging on the ledge a bit today, but we'll pick up tomorrow; I want this truth to simmer a bit before we go any further.

God Is . . . LOVE

Day 2

All scripture is congruent and supports what has already been declared. So, what does the Bible tell us about love?

> Love is patient and kind; love does not envy or boast; it is not arrogant or rude. It does not insist on its own way; it is not irritable or resentful; it does not rejoice at wrongdoing, but rejoices with the truth. Love bears all things, believes all things, hopes all things, endures all things.
>
> (1 Corinthians 13:4–7 ESV)

Since God is love, and 1 Corinthians 13 gives us a detailed description of love, this scripture must also be a detailed description of who God is. Do you see God in this list of descriptors? Is God patient? Is He kind? Yes, He is because He is love!

I recall God's patience with me when I struggled with cigarette addiction. I smoked two packs every day. I knew my body was His temple, I knew it was bad for my health, and I knew it was not God's best life for me. Some days I fought the urge, and other days I didn't even try to fight it. On both occasions, God was patient with me and showed His kindness toward me.

Does God infringe on our free will by insisting on His own way? Does He glory in sin and wrongdoing? He does not, and, more important, He cannot because He is love. Although both God and I knew that living under the bondage of nicotine addiction was not His will or His best for me, love does not insist on having its own way. God continued to compel me to change, He continued to offer me a way out, but the choice was mine alone to make.

Now, please don't mistake God's grace and His patience for acceptance and approval! Because He is love, God does not glory in sin and wrongdoing. His grace gave me time and opportunity to choose freedom from bondage through a relationship with Him, but while I was receiving His grace, He never once put Himself in agreement with my choice to live in bondage.

God is love, and He sent Himself in the form of the Son to die for us. The Son sends Himself—love—after us every day. When we hide in shame, love comes to find us. When we run in fear, love chases us down. Aren't you glad that He won't ever stop coming after you? His love is relentless. He will continue to be patient and kind, but He will never align Himself with sin in our lives. Instead, He will send love to passionately pursue each of us until love wins us over.

God Is . . . LOVE
Day 3

Have you ever viewed God apart from love? I recommend studying the Word of God, specifically scriptures that reveal His nature. Pray the prayer below and praise God for being love!

Patient and grace-giving God, today I praise You for Your love that never runs out! You are relentless in Your love pursuit of me, and I could never thank You enough for how You continue to come after me. Through times of struggle, times of complacency, and even times of out-right rebellion, You patiently sought after a relationship with me. You never condoned my choices, but because Your love for me runs deep, You also never condemned me. God, You don't love me because of who I am; rather, You love me because love is who You are; and for that, I pause and respond with a heart of gratitude. As aware as I am of Your love for me, I know that I am still unable to fully comprehend the depths and the width of this unconditional, never-ceasing, life-giving love. My prayer today is that I live out my days reciprocating the love You give me by living a life of obedience to Your Word. It is in the precious name of Jesus Christ I pray.

Amen.

At some point today, continue this exercise on the next by journaling your own prayer of praise for His patient love in your life.

God Is . . . LOVE

Prayer Journal

God Is . . . LOVE

Day 4

Today's #QOTD is from world-renowned evangelist, Billy Graham.

"God proved His love on the cross. When Christ hung, and bled, and died, it was God saying to the world, 'I love you.'"[4]

Today's #SOTD is "Reckless Love" by Cory Asbury. As always, use this space to journal your thoughts, feelings, and reflections after reading this quote and hearing this song.

_____
_____
_____
_____
_____
_____
_____
_____
_____
_____
_____
_____

God Is . . . LOVE
Day 5

Today is a day of reflection. Use the space below to record how God's love chased you down until He won you over. Recall those times in your life when you felt undeserving of love from this all-knowing God, yet His love for you never ceased. This is your space to write your story. *Your story matters.* Your testimony of how His love won you over might just be the story that helps someone else overcome one day.

_____

_____

_____

_____

_____

_____

_____

_____

_____

_____

_____

_____

_____

_____

_____

_____

God Is . . . LOVE

Day 6

Clue 1:

I was a young shepherd boy whose family never thought I'd be much else.

Clue 2:

I was anointed king yet continued to serve as a meager sheep herder until God's appointed time.

Clue 3:

I lost focus on God and committed a vile act of sexual sin with a married woman, had her husband murdered to cover it up, yet I still experienced the unfailing love of God. That love redeemed and restored me.

Who am I? _____

God Is . . . LOVE

Day 7

Selah

The Christian does not think God will love us because we are good, but that God will make us good because He loves us.

C. S. Lewis

You don't have to be good enough to earn God's love. Love is who God is, and as He pursues us with love, His goal is to win us over to a life of obedience so that His love can make us good. Pause and rest in that truth today.

_____

_____

_____

_____

_____

_____

_____

_____

_____

_____

_____

Week 5: God Is . . . MY REDEEMER

Day 1

But it is because the Lord loves you and is keeping the oath that he swore to your fathers, that the Lord has brought you out with a mighty hand and redeemed you from the house of slavery, from the hand of Pharaoh king of Egypt.

Deuteronomy 7:8 (ESV)

According to the *Holman Bible Dictionary*, a redeemer, in our spotlight scripture for today, is derived from the Hebrew custom of buying something back. Now, this object is something that formerly belonged to the purchaser, but for some reason, it has passed into the ownership of another. The original owner could regain ownership of the item, but it would require them to pay a redemption price for it. Whoa! If you are like me, you just saw your life story play out in that definition.

We were created in the image and likeness of God, for God, and belonging to God. However, our sin nature and our lusts drew us away from Him (James 1:14), and we each became servants of another. Even if we never considered ourselves wicked or evil people, our lives were not being used for the purpose in which we were created. Our ownership had passed to the Enemy of our souls, and he conspired to kill us while in his possession. But God is our Redeemer. Jesus voluntarily came to earth and paid the price for our sins and removed the wrath of God against us. His death on the cross, His shed blood, and His bludgeoned and broken body was the only sufficient redemption price for our lives and our souls. His unwarranted death redeemed us by paying the redemption price, and this redemption makes everything about us new.

How many movies have you seen in which someone's child was abducted? What is one of the first things police officers tell the parents? "The first forty-eight hours are crucial. Let's set up a phone line in your home in case the abductor reaches out, demanding a ransom."

Me as the parent of the abducted child talking to the abductor: "Why in the world would I pay you for something that already belongs to me? This child is mine. I created him, I care for him, I provide for him! You don't even love or want this child; you just want whatever you can get out of me. You have *stolen* my child and now you have the nerve to demand a redemption price."

Also me: "Now, who do I make this check payable to again?"

Why would I, or any parent, even consider paying the ransom? Because when something, in this case, someone, is valuable to us, we are willing to pay the price. We are valuable to Christ—that's why He willingly laid down His life to buy us back.

God Is . . . MY REDEEMER
Day 2

I paused and took a moment to really understand what it means to call God my Redeemer. I was created by God. I belonged to God, and I was His precious possession. Then I lost my mother to lupus. Because I was not assured of the irrevocable truth of God's nature, I became discontent with belonging to Him. I was drawn away from Him by my own evil desires to deal with pain outside of His love and comfort. What was once precious and possessed by the Father was now lost and broken. I was bound by addiction. I was desperate for something that could heal the deep hurt in my heart, and I turned to temporary relief like cigarettes and alcohol.

One night, at a party I was hosting, I came to understand that I had left something eternal for something temporary; that the Enemy had hoodwinked me into believing the lie that immediate was better than infinite. Nevertheless, God is my Redeemer, and He came after me that night. I was drunk as a skunk (still had the bottle of vodka in my hand) when I cried out to God and asked Him if it was too late for me. I pleaded with God to take me back and give me another chance. At that moment, the Lord spoke sweetly and reminded me that Christ's death had long ago paid the required price for my sin. Knowing that I would leave the relationship His blood paid for, Christ still gave His life so that at the moment I decided I was available again, He could buy me back to Himself!

He is waiting, longing to do the same for each of His children. Come out of the corner of condemnation. With a broken spirit and a sorrowful heart, make yourself available to the Father again. As soon as you place yourself on the shelf of availability, He will lovingly remind you that the redemption price was already paid.

God Is . . . MY REDEEMER
Day 3

Today, pray the prayer below to both acknowledge and accept God as your Redeemer. No matter where you are in your walk with Christ (even if that journey has yet to begin), this prayer is always in order.

Merciful God, I know You love me and You sent Your only Son to die in my stead. My sin, my choice to lose satisfaction in You, passed my ownership to the Enemy of my soul and I am so sorry. I ask Your forgiveness. I recognize my need for You not only as my Savior but also as the Lord of my life. I know that Your holy standard is impossible to reach in my own strength. I realize that my merit will never be enough, and without Christ I would be separated from You for all eternity. So I pray that You redeem me now. Buy me back to You with Your redemptive blood and fill me with more of Your Spirit. Assure me that I am forever redeemed as I walk in fellowship with You each day. I trust You not to let me be put to shame. Show me Your ways and teach me Your paths. It is in the redemptive name of Jesus Christ I pray.

Amen.

At some point today, continue this exercise on the next page by journaling your own prayer of how your life changed (or will change) when you returned home to your rightful owner.

God Is . . . MY REDEEMER
Prayer Journal

God Is . . . MY REDEEMER

Day 4

Today's #QOTD is from British writer and theologian C.S. Lewis.

"The Son of God became a man to enable men to become sons of God."[5]

Today's #SOTD is "Rescue" by Lauren Daigle. Of course, use this space to journal your thoughts, feelings, and reflections after reading this quote and hearing this song.

_____
_____
_____
_____
_____
_____
_____
_____
_____
_____
_____
_____
_____
_____

God Is . . . MY REDEEMER
Day 5

Today is a day of reflection. Use the space below to record the redemption power of God that has rescued you and made you new. You might compare and contrast your life before you accepted Christ's redemption versus the transformation His blood has made in you. You might also choose to recall what you've been redeemed from and what you're *redeemed for*! What purpose has His redemption unlocked in your heart?

_____
_____
_____
_____
_____
_____
_____
_____
_____
_____
_____
_____
_____
_____
_____
_____

God Is . . . MY REDEEMER

Day 6

Clue 1:

I was a promiscuous woman who was guilty of numerous sexual sins, including prostitution.

Clue 2:

At the Lord's instruction, my husband came and found me, married me, and fathered my children, although I continually broke our marriage vows by returning to my ways of harlotry.

Clue 3:

My infidelity was a symbol of Israel's spiritual unfaithfulness, but my husband's, Hosea, marriage and faithfulness to me is an enduring symbol of God's faithfulness and provisional redemption of His unfaithful people, then and now, through Jesus Christ.

Who am I? _____

God Is . . . MY REDEEMER

Day 7

Selah

Have you ever felt that your mistakes and life choices wrote a price tag that Jesus would not want to pay for you? Believe this truth: Jesus paid the price once and for all on the cross. If you would simply make yourself available to Him again, you, too, can know Him as Redeemer. If you have already accepted this gift of redemption, be assured of your newness in Christ. His blood was enough for you! I encourage you to be intentional in spending time being mindful of this truth today.

Week 6: God Is . . . My Shepherd

Day 1

The LORD is my shepherd; I shall not want.

Psalm 23:1 (KJV)

To fully understand the metaphorical phrase "The Lord is my shepherd," we must first understand that if He is the shepherd, this makes us His sheep. Even a brief study on sheep reveals the tendency of sheep to wander off and get lost. One of my favorite hymns, "Come Thou Fount", eloquently expresses our sheep-like nature when it says, "Prone to wander, Lord I feel it. Prone to leave the God I love." When we fail to allow the Spirit of God to serve as our Shepherd and guide, we are highly inclined to wander off from the fold of God. It is our nature to drift away, to break God's commands, and to reject His righteousness, which is why we so desperately need Him as our shepherd.

The author of this psalm, David, understood in detail what it meant to call someone a shepherd. Although anointed king at a young age, David continued to serve as a shepherd to his father's flocks of sheep. From his experience, David knew that to call the Lord his shepherd meant to call the Lord a protector, a guide, a provider, a physician, and a savior. There is good news in all of this: God takes delight in caring for and providing the needs of His fold (His children). He is aware of our proclivity to wander off or to become easily distracted and lose sight of the path He's taking us down. So, with patience He guides us. With strength, He wards off danger. With kindness, He corrects our missteps, and with grace, He continues to call out to us, guiding us to our destiny.

God Is . . . My Shepherd
Day 2

I can recall numerous occasions when I strayed from the Lord's leading as my shepherd. A specific instance that is forever etched on the tablets of my heart occurred a few years ago. My work environment had gotten toxic that I found it very difficult to enjoy the very important work we did. I felt unheard and undervalued as an employee. I prayed for guidance about finding new work and where I should go next. Being the Good Shepherd and knowing what was ahead, God guided me right back to that same dreary place of employment week after week. Honestly, I became frustrated with God's timeline and even questioned His ability to lead me. Outside of His direction, I applied for jobs that I was over-qualified for, jobs that were perfect for my skill set. But I received no call backs and no interviews. Filled to the brim with apathy, I walked into my office one day. A coworker with whom I laughed a lot with came into my office and closed the door behind her. Her demeanor was very different from our routine of how's-it-going and joke-telling. With tear-filled eyes, she said, "I've been a Jehovah's Witness my entire life, but the light in you that shines for Jesus has sparked my curiosity. Can you tell me about your faith?"

Of course, now we're crying together. For weeks we talked about Jesus—His love for humanity, His plan for each of us, and what it means to live relationally with Him. Our shepherd had left the ninety-nine sheep to come after the lost one (see Luke 15:3–7), and my proclivity to wander almost delayed His plan.

God Is . . . My Shepherd

After about six weeks of our conversations about Jesus and her going to a Christian church, she came into my office early one Monday morning to tell me she had committed her life to Jesus over the weekend. What sweet restoration to my soul to hear those words! The shepherd had a plan far better than mine. And as if that wasn't enough, I received a phone call the next day to interview for a job I had applied for more than ten times before! As I recommitted myself to my position as His sheep and allowed Him to be the shepherd guide of my life, I saw just how trustworthy our God is.

God Is . . . My Shepherd
Day 3

Today, pray the prayer below to remind yourself of God's direction over your life.

God, my Good Shepherd, I am reminded today that You lead each moment of my life. You desire that I follow the path You have laid out before me. Although I cannot always see the next step, I am confident, because of Your nature, that each next one leads to joy and contentment. So, Lord, I pray that You continue to guide my life and give me discernment as I move forward while trusting you. In moments when I lack wisdom, I pray that You increase Your wisdom in me. Teach me not to worry about tomorrow, or next week, or next year. You provide for the birds and for the lilies, and You've promised to always provide for those of us crafted in Your own image. My prayer today is that I never rush through my morning routine without consulting You about where You will lead me. May I never make a move without Your direction. Nevertheless, if I falter, I pray You will redirect me with Your rod and staff to realign me with Your divine will. It is in the trustworthy name of Jesus Christ I pray.

Amen.

At some point today, continue this exercise on the next page by journaling your own prayer.

God Is . . . My Shepherd

Prayer Journal

_____
_____
_____
_____
_____
_____
_____
_____
_____
_____
_____
_____
_____
_____
_____
_____

God Is . . . My Shepherd

Day 4

Today's #QOTD is from best-selling Christian author and pastor Max Lucado.

"You need to know what you have in your Shepherd. You have a God who hears you, the power of love behind you, the Holy Spirit within you, and all of heaven ahead of you. If you have the Shepherd, you have grace for every sin, direction for every turn, a candle for every corner, and an anchor for every storm. You have everything you need!"[6]

Today's #SOTD is "Psalm 23" by People & Songs. Of course, use this space to journal your thoughts, feelings, and reflections after reading this quote and hearing this song.

_____
_____
_____
_____
_____
_____
_____
_____
_____

God Is . . . My Shepherd

Day 5

Today is a day of reflection. Use the space below to record how and when you have experienced our God as a protector, a guide, a provider, a physician—a shepherd.

_____
_____
_____
_____
_____
_____
_____
_____
_____
_____
_____
_____
_____
_____
_____
_____
_____
_____
_____

God Is . . . My Shepherd

Day 6

Clue 1:

I tried to run away after being caught in my sin, but the angel of the Lord came and spoke to me on Mount Horeb.

Clue 2:

God gave me a task that seemed much too large for me to handle, but He provided guidance and provision each step of the way.

Clue 3:

As I followed God's leading, I saw miracle after miracle for myself and the people God asked me to set free. He provided for us in the wilderness, parted the sea for us to cross over, swallowed up our enemies, and guided us to the land He had promised.

Who am I? _____

God Is . . . My Shepherd

Day 7

Selah

Stop trying to do life your way. That thing you have been doing to "force fix" your situation without God's clear direction? Stop. Relax. Rest in Him. Give the reigns back to God and allow Him to be *your* shepherd. Consider those areas of your life where you have moved out on your own without the guidance of God. Pray and listen for His voice as He guides you back to green pastures and still waters. I encourage you to be intentional in spending time being mindful of this truth today.

Week 7: God Is . . . PEACE

Day 1

For the mountains may be removed and the hills may shake, but My lovingkindness will not be removed from you, nor will My covenant of peace be shaken," says the Lord who has compassion on you.

Isaiah 54:10 AMP

We often walk through difficult or frustrating situations and ask for or wait on God's peace. When a circumstance flusters us, we plead with God and recall His Word to Him during our prayer time. "Lord, You promised You'd keep me in perfect peace. Lord, give me peace that passes all of my understanding." The reality is, no matter how tumultuous our lives feel at times, His covenant of peace will not be shaken (Isaiah 54:10). God is a covenant-keeping God! He has an absolute inability to lie. When He sets Himself in agreement with something, it is established. And He has set Himself in agreement with our living and walking in peace. Regardless of what is going on around us, peace is available within us. Isaiah 26:3 says, "You will keep in perfect peace all who trust in you, all whose thoughts are fixed on you!" (NLT). This is a promise from our God.

However, many of us find ourselves exasperated by life because we fail to adhere to our end of the deal. Our responsibility is to trust God to set our thoughts on Him. We must make a conscious choice to reject our desire to fixate on the problem and, instead, turn our hearts and attention to God, completely confident that He will both calm the storm and provide peace in the process. This prerequisite is what qualifies us to be kept in the perfect peace of God.

God Is . . . PEACE
Day 2

Have you ever been juggling so many balls at once that you are consumed with anxiety, anticipating the moment that they will all come crashing to the ground?

For a period of time during 2018, this is how I felt, fearing I would drop those balls of my daily activities and responsibilities and leave me standing with both hands in the air. Would you believe me if I told you that both hands in the air is the perfect position to receive the peace of God?

I had a routine: I woke up, and before I even spoke to God or brushed my teeth, I was writing my mental to-do list. After I had prioritized my day, drank my coffee (venti caramel macchiato, quad, with extra caramel drizzle), applied my everyday face, and slipped on a maxi dress that I had already worn once since its last wash, I stopped and asked God for His presence in and guidance through my day.

Looking back, I can clearly see how contradictory it was for me to decide my day and then ask God to guide me. But at the time, asking for His guidance was honestly just part of my daily to-do that came after coffee and mascara. Before long, I was overextended, underperforming, and out of fellowship with the God of peace whom I was in desperate need of.

Do you know what I did? I kept my hands up, took a step back, and let it all come crashing down! I took my hands off of my agenda, my ambitions, my to-do lists, and my anxiety, but I kept my hands up. I kept them lifted to God as a sign of surrender and, an expression of repentance and regret for benching Him while I tried to be the entire starting line-up for my life. I decided to keep my hands up and receive the peace that Jesus spoke of in John 14. But before I could receive that peace, I made the decision that my heart would not be troubled or afraid. I would not fear how I would catch up on life if I re-prioritized Jesus in His rightful place—as the head of my life and the orchestrator of each day. Instead, I rested in His peace and knew that our covenant-keeping God would help me to pick up each responsibility again, and through consistent fellowship with Him, I could keep every necessary thing in the air all while abiding in His unshakable peace.

God Is . . . PEACE
Day 3

Today, pray the prayer below to remind yourself that you are responsible to keep your mind on your trustworthy God as He keeps you in perfect peace.

Covenant-keeping God of peace, I stop all my busyness and recognize You as a God who cannot lie. You promised to keep me in perfect peace as I trust and fix my heart on You. I realize how I have allowed my tasks, jobs, and activities to precede fellowship with You. I repent for dethroning You in my life, and I ask that You return to Your place as the King of my heart. I pray that You sit at the helm of my heart and direct my life as You see fit. Lord, teach me to trust Your priorities for my life. Teach me to seek You for guidance before I commit myself. Father, give me renewed strength to align my will with Yours and persist in what You assign to my hands. May I never feel alone in accomplishing the assignment, but make me ever aware that it is only through You that I am able to live in peace regardless of what is happening around me. I trust You, and I realign my heart with Your plan for me. It is in the sure name of Jesus Christ I pray.

Amen.

At some point today, continue this exercise on the next page by journaling your own prayer.

God Is . . . PEACE

Prayer Journal

_____
_____
_____
_____
_____
_____
_____
_____
_____
_____
_____
_____
_____
_____
_____
_____

God Is . . . PEACE

Day 4

Today's #QOTD is from fifteenth-century theologian Martin Luther.

"I have held many things in my hands, and have lost them all; but whatever I have placed in God's hands, that I still possess."[7]

Today's #SOTD is "By Myself" by Deon Kipping. Of course, us this space to journal your thoughts, feelings, and reflections after reading this quote and hearing this song.

_____
_____
_____
_____
_____
_____
_____
_____
_____
_____
_____
_____

God Is . . . PEACE

Day 5

Today is a day of reflection. Use the space below to record anything you have prioritized above the God of peace in your life. How will you realign your heart with His?

God Is . . . PEACE

Day 6

Clue 1:

We were pestered by a woman possessed by evil spirits as we journeyed to the place of prayer. After many days of enduring the frustration this caused, we turned and rebuked the spirit from her.

Clue 2:

After rebuking the spirit from the possessed woman, we were taken before Roman officials who had us stripped, flogged and thrown in jail for preaching in the name of Jesus in a Roman city.

Clue 3:

Frustrated, overwhelmed, bound, and tired, we lifted our hands and voices in praise to God in the midst of our storm. At that moment, despite what we were facing, God's peace overwhelmed us and even freed us from prison.

Who are we? _____

God Is . . . PEACE

Day 7

Selah

If you are feeling overwhelmed today, I encourage you to let all your busyness, work, activities, and responsibilities come crashing down! Step back and reconnect with your God, who is peace. Be sure to keep your hands up. Sit quietly today and be intentional in spending time being mindful of this truth.

Week 8: God Is . . . THE WELL!

Day 1

Everyone who thirsts, come to the waters;
And you who have no money come, buy grain and eat.
Come, buy wine and milk
Without money and without cost [simply accept it as a gift from God].

Isaiah 55:1 (AMP)

Fear the LORD, you his godly people, for those who fear him will have all they need.

Psalm 34:9 (NLT)

In Isaiah 55, we receive an invitation from the God of the universe to "come." Those of us who are thirsty, those of us who are lacking and in need, we are invited to receive from our all-sufficient God, who never runs out. We are summoned to partake in the thing we have the greatest need of and, without cost consider it a gift from a God who houses endless pleasures at His right hand. *Come!*

When we honor and reverence God appropriately in our lives, we are able to come and receive all that we need in Him. We don't just receive it *from Him*, but we receive it *in Him*. Many times we glue our

God Is . . . THE WELL!

eyes on our "life-clock," and second by second the days pass and we conclude that God is not supplying what we need. However, I have learned that often-times the things we go without either we don't truly have need of them, or they are things we are looking for outside of Him. It's not our God's nature to invite us to waters that will dry up or run out. Leave your logic and come. Stop looking to things and people in your life who were meant to be resources and come to God who is the source of all you need. Come to the well that never runs dry. God is the well!

God Is . . . THE WELL!
Day 2

The truth is, when we spot deficiency in our lives, it is likely that we need more of God than we need more of the things that are deficient. He is a never-ending supply of what is lacking in our lives! He is the well; He serves as the source and every other stream is simply a resource.

Could it be that we have filled our minds and hearts with searching for acceptance when God has already justified us (Romans 8:30)? Sometimes we feel that joy is lacking in our lives, so we look to friends to make us happy. But the truth is, our joy is full and complete in Him (John 15:11). Although people can be a great blessing from God, they were never intended to replace God as the one who is able to provide our needs. Often, it's not until we recognize that the fumes that have been keeping us chugging along are almost gone, that we run to God for help. The truth is, we never had to get that low; we never had to chance burnout because we serve God, who is a well of abundant supply. What need can we have that our Father cannot provide? Nothing!

I can remember the first six months after my dad died as being six of the most fulfilled months I have lived to date. In a time when my joy was waning, peace seemed far away, and purpose was foggier than ever. I was *empty*. I had no encouraging card, no song of praise or worship that seemed able to fill me. Then I remembered that all these streams were simply resources, and what I needed was the source of

God Is . . . THE WELL!

endless supply. I needed something beyond momentary relief, something greater than a quick mental reprieve. I needed something constant and unending. It was during these six months that I clung to God. I was not able to come with an offering; I came in search of something. Each day, sometimes multiple times throughout the day, I came with my empty bucket, begging God to fill me again, to increase my strength, to restore my peace of mind, and to heal my broken places. Each time I let my bucket down into the well of His presence, He filled it to the brim. And because I came in response to His standing invitation, there was no guilt or shame. I was in His presence by invitation, and He renewed and restored me. I was filled to overflowing from this well of Living Water. God is the well, and He is beckoning *you* to come and drink.

God Is . . . THE WELL!
Day 3

Today, pray the prayer below as your acceptance of His invitation to come and receive from Him.

All-sufficient King, I come to You now as Your child. I come without guilt or shame because You have invited me to come when I am running low or even when I am completely empty. You invite me to come without anything to trade or offer, so here I am. I believe that Your sufficiency is always greater than my need. You are a never-ending well, and You do not run dry. I pray that Your sufficiency will be my supply today and always. Help me always look to You as my source. Help me to recognize every other person and thing in my life as a resource that extends from Your abundant grace. Your presence is always enough to satisfy. It is in the victorious name of Jesus Christ I pray and ask it all.

Amen.

At some point today, continue this exercise on the next page by journaling your own prayer.

God Is . . . THE WELL!
Prayer Journal

God Is . . . THE WELL!

Day 4

Today's #QOTD is from author Sylvia Gunter.

"Our lack is perfectly engineered to magnify His perfect sufficiency."[8]

Today's #SOTD is "The Isaiah Song" by All Nations Worship Assembly Atlanta. Of course, use this space to journal your thoughts, feelings, and reflections after reading this quote and hearing this song.

_____
_____
_____
_____
_____
_____
_____
_____
_____
_____
_____
_____
_____
_____

God Is . . . THE WELL!
Day 5

Today is a day of reflection. Use the space below to record the times in your life when you went to the well empty and He filled you to the brim. May this record serve as your forever reminder that your all-sufficient God is more than enough.

_____
_____
_____
_____
_____
_____
_____
_____
_____
_____
_____
_____
_____
_____
_____
_____
_____
_____
_____
_____
_____
_____

God Is . . . THE WELL!

Day 6

Clue 1:

I was gathering sticks in Zarephath when the prophet Elijah came into town and asked me for water and bread.

Clue 2:

The truth is, I had only a little flour and very little oil. I had planned to make one final meal for me and me my son that day. We would eat that meal together and then die from lack.

Clue 3:

As an act of obedience, I made the prophet's meal first. Little did I know that this small act would lead me to the well of our all-sufficient God, who would meet and exceed my family's need by causing our supply of flour and oil to overflow.

Who am I? _____

God Is . . . THE WELL!

Day 7

Selah

Are you running low today? Prioritize God's presence. Accept His invitation to come to the well and draw from Him. He is all-sufficient God. I encourage you to be intentional in spending time being mindful of this truth today.

Week 9: God Is . . . A REFINER

Day 1

*And he shall sit as a refiner and purifier of silver: and he shall purify the sons of Levi, and purge them as gold and silver, that they may offer unto the L*ORD *an offering in righteousness.*

Malachi 3:3 (KJV)

Have you ever been in a place where you felt like God turned up the heat in your life? Especially as a believer, sometimes those seemingly extreme difficulties feel unfair. If we are honest, we know that persecution and tribulation are inevitable parts of life, but in those times when we are giving God our very best, challenges can make us raise an eyebrow to God and question, Why? Do you love me? Are you really for me? What's the plan here?

The answer to your why is simple: the fire refines us. The best news found in this truth is that our Father is the refiner. He is the one responsible to determine the appropriate temperature for the refinement of each precious metal. As believers, we do not have to fear fiery trails and afflictions because we can stand assured that our God, the refiner, knows the intensity necessary to reveal the precious gifts He placed inside of us. Trials won't be more intense than necessary, and they won't last a second longer than is required to get the good stuff out of us. Refinement is the purification process believers undergo to remove all undesirable characteristics and reveal those that God deems most desirable. The refiner sits on the throne of our hearts and orders the events of our lives to purify us and make us more like Him.

God Is . . . A REFINER
Day 2

I'm not one to wear my messes like a badge of honor, but don't be fooled, I have my fair share. I love God and I work to live submitted to His desires for me, but there are still some undesirable characteristics in me that the refiner is purifying.

I can remember attending a women's conference and doing a group exercise with the other ladies at my table. I felt as if one of those activities was intended to awaken emotion and possibly provoke tears. It started with a long introduction reminding us of how loving our God is and how He sees us with eyes of love regardless of what our pasts have been. The speaker repeatedly shared how God's eyes of grace cause Him to call us something totally different from what our circumstances, our peers and our habits call us. The instructor then posed this question: "Regardless of who or what you were in your past, when God looks at you, what does He call you?"

Women at my table began to share heartfelt words of affirmation as they choked on their tears. "Friend, God sees me and He calls me friend." "He calls me beloved!" "Wanted, God still says I am wanted."

Now, it's my turn. I tried to pretend that I was shy as I asked softly to be skipped. The truth was, I knew that what I wrote down as my answer was nothing like the other answers being shared. These women of God rallied around me and encouraged me, coached me, and even prayed for me to have the courage to "Speak your truth, sister." So, glance at what I had written on my note card, and said confidently, "Hot mess! God looks at me and calls me a hot mess!"

After what seemed to be minutes of absolute stunned silence, laughter erupted in the room. Every woman at that table admitted that this was the word they should have written on their cards. I knew that God called me *friend* and *beloved* and *chosen* and even *wanted*, but I was also mindful that God was well aware of the "hot mess" in me that still needed to be refined.

Daily, God sits on the throne of my heart and causes fiery trials to purify me. He allows some storms to bring the worst of me to the surface so that I become more aware of its existence in me. Then, by His grace and His power, He strengthens me to remove the mess by my increasing dependence on Him. As He continues to separate the desirable from the undesirable, He is more able to see His reflection in the precious people He is refining: His children!

God Is . . . A REFINER

Day 3

Today, pray the prayer below asking God to help you accept the process of purification and refinement, even when the heat is turned up in your life.

Gracious God, I am grateful that You see all of my flaws and failures yet You choose to call me friend. I also recognize that Your grace does not cause You to become content with the parts of me that do not please You. For this reason, You sit as the refiner of my life and heart. You allow Your Word, life circumstances, and even my decisions to bring undesirable characteristics to the surface so that You can purify me. I am a work in progress! I don't use that as an excuse to opt out of continual growth; today, I say that as a declaration that I am allowing the work to happen. I am embracing the process of progress even in moments of difficulty. Today, I am deciding to allow You to use fiery trials as a means of purifying me.

Above all, I want to be more like You, Lord. Separate the undesirable traits from those in me that most reflect Your goodness and Your glory. I am Yours, and I trust You with my life. It is in the righteous name of Jesus Christ I pray.

Amen.

At some point today, continue this exercise on the next page by journaling your own prayer.

God Is . . . A REFINER
Prayer Journal

God Is . . . A REFINER

Day 4

Today's #QOTD is from pastor, author, and renowned teacher John Piper.

"He is a refiner's fire, and that makes all the difference. A refiner's fire does not destroy indiscriminately like a forest fire. A refiner's fire does not consume completely like the fire of an incinerator. A refiner's fire refines. It purifies. It melts down the bar of silver or gold, separates out the impurities that ruin its value, burns them up, and leaves the silver and gold intact. He is like a refiner's fire."[9]

Today's #SOTD is "You Keep Me" by Travis Greene. Of course, use this space to journal your thoughts, feelings, and reflections after reading this quote and hearing this song.

_____
_____
_____
_____
_____
_____
_____
_____

God Is . . . A REFINER

Day 5

Today is a day of reflection. Use the space below to record the times in your life when God used the fiery days of trial or trouble to make you better. Maybe you didn't realize it at the moment, but think through those times with openness and search for areas of growth. May this record serve as your proof that He causes *all things* to work together for good as He refines you.

_____
_____
_____
_____
_____
_____
_____
_____
_____
_____
_____
_____
_____
_____
_____
_____

God Is . . . A REFINER

Day 6

Clue 1:

I lived at home with my dad, my older brother, and many of my family's servants.

Clue 2:

One day I decided that I wanted to receive my inheritance from my father. Although it was not customary for me to ask, nor for my father to oblige, he did. He gave me my portion, and I left for a far-away country.

Clue 3:

I was living my best life until I ran out of money. It all started piling up so quickly: my friends left, my money was gone, and there was even a food shortage in my town. I got a job feeding pigs. The day I considered eating what the pigs ate, I knew it was time to return home. When I did, my father gladly welcomed me back and restored my dignity. The way my father honored me, despite my shortcomings, was amazing. I am a better person having experienced this.

Who am I? _____

God Is . . . A REFINER

Day 7

Selah

Does it seem like it's all piling up? Does life seem unfair? Do you feel like there is no real purpose to the difficulty you've been enduring? Pause. Breathe. Remember, it's a process, and if you allow it, it will make you better. It doesn't mean you deserve it; it just means it's happening and all you can do is choose how you will respond. I encourage you to respond by trusting God to make something beautiful emerge from the ashes. I encourage you to be intentional in spending time being mindful of this truth today.

Week 10: God Is . . . A GOOD RECORD KEEPER

Day 1

Whatever you do, work at it with all your heart, as working for the Lord, not for human masters, since you know that you will receive an inheritance from the Lord as a reward. It is the Lord Christ you are serving.

Colossians 3:23–24

That thine alms may be in secret: and thy Father which seeth in secret himself shall reward thee openly.

Matthew 6:4 (KJV)

The verse from Colossians 3 spoke specifically to servants during that time. Their instruction was that as they are serving their masters, they should mind their attitude. They were not to serve solely out of obligation or necessity but to serve with good intent and will. The charge then went a step further by instructing them to serve, not as if they were doing it *for God*, but as if their service was *to God*.

This principle should govern each act of service we fill our lives with. Our intent should always be good and the aim of our efforts reserved completely for Christ. It would be hypocritical of us to do the works of God while looking for the praises of people. If vain praise from others is our motivation when serving, that praise is our due reward. As we serve God through acts of obedience in our personal lives or through

God Is . . . A GOOD RECORD KEEPER

service to others, we must do them only to be approved by God. Then when we truly offer ourselves, gifts, networks, resources, time, and treasures to God without expectation, it positions us for favor and reward from the Lord. This is not to say that our acts deserve His favor, but in His grace, He grants it to us as a reward.

God Is . . . A GOOD RECORD KEEPER
Day 2

Today's message is for everyone serving God under the radar. I don't mean those who keep quiet about their faith. I mean those who serve without desiring to be noticed, or celebrated, or invited to the front, or approved by people. Keep serving your God. Keep loving His people well. Keep interceding, keep leading worship, keep shepherding people, keep cleaning the toilets, and keep greeting visitors with a warm smile. Whatever capacity you serve in, continue. I realize that this goes against most of our natural proclivities. As humans, we desire to be loved and appreciated and accepted, but don't let those desires drive your service. Let every act and deed, every word and endeavor be rooted in humility, drenched in goodness, and offered only to our Father.

I struggled for years with my identity in Christ, and because I wasn't secure in who I was created to be, I needed validation and approval from those for whom I performed. Receiving compliments and encouragement after ministering, I would feel affirmed and approved—until the next time. The words were always fleeting; they were never enough to permanently keep my insecurities at bay.

Then one day, I received words of wisdom I will never forget. "Victoria, do what you do as unto the Lord. You minister to an audience of one. You don't need anyone's validation. He has justified you. Serve God by serving His people well, and remember, He's a good record keeper." Those words settled me at that moment, and they have grounded me for years. I began to serve God differently. My acts of service became acts of worship reserved solely for Christ the Lord. I didn't need anyone to celebrate me when I stepped off the stage. Actually, I began to forsake the stage. You see, performers stand on stages. They perform their routine and then wait for validation and approval through audience response. I'd had enough of that, so I decided never to step foot on another stage. Instead, I would consciously renounce pride and arrogance. I gave my ego no room, and I abandoned insecurities. Every stage became an altar where my worship could ascend to God. The reward has been incredible. Yes, the opportunities and the networks have been a true blessing, but the greatest reward has been the freedom from fear and the closeness with my Creator. I invite you today to forsake the stage and cling to the altar. Make or renew your commitment to do everything with all of your heart. Don't seek attention, fame, or approval from others—God is taking good notes, and by His grace, your reward is on the way!

God Is . . . A GOOD RECORD KEEPER

Day 3

Today, pray the prayer below asking God to start and keep you on a path that glorifies Him through your acts of love and service.

Lord Jesus, You are the meaning of all of life. You are the only one worth giving myself to and for. No one and nothing could ever bring that fulfilment and sense of belonging that You offer. May you be the goal of all my desires, the satisfaction of all my longings, and the end of all my work. Help me, by Your Holy Spirit, to seek and find You in all that I do. Lord, I want to be a faithful disciple and responsible steward of all that You've entrusted to me. Teach me to serve faithfully. Reenergize me to continually build altars when society would have me erect a stage. May I live for an audience of one—You, Lord! Reignite me by Your Spirit that I may serve with a grateful, generous, and responsible heart. It's in the worthy name of Jesus Christ I pray and ask it all.

Amen.

At some point today, continue this exercise on the next page by journaling your own prayer.

God Is . . . A GOOD RECORD KEEPER

Prayer Journal

God Is . . . A GOOD RECORD KEEPER

Day 4

Today's #QOTD is from my spiritual mentor and pastor, Cheryl Rice.

"Our God is a good record keeper."

Today's #SOTD is "This Altar" by Psalmist Raine. Of course, use this space to journal your thoughts, feelings, and reflections after reading this quote and hearing this song.

_____
_____
_____
_____
_____
_____
_____
_____
_____
_____
_____
_____
_____
_____
_____
_____

God Is . . . A GOOD RECORD KEEPER
Day 5

Today is a day of reflection. Use the space below to denote the areas in your life where you have forsaken the stage and clung to the altar. How did you feel? What have been the greatest rewards from your faithfulness? May this record serve as your reminder that He is watching, and He's taking good notes! He rewards faithfulness!

_____
_____
_____
_____
_____
_____
_____
_____
_____
_____
_____
_____
_____
_____
_____
_____
_____

God Is . . . A GOOD RECORD KEEPER

Day 6

Clue 1:

I was not afraid of being politically incorrect, and I was not looking for people to approve or validate me in what I did for God.

Clue 2:

I was never one who longed for attention or celebration from other people. I was always pretty aware of my life's purpose and wanted to spend my days doing what I was sent to do so that I could please the God who sent me.

Clue 3:

My faithfulness in serving God paid off in such a great way. Maybe not in the way that most people expect reward and recompense, but for me, it was truly a gift. I was able to experience a closeness with Jesus that no one else ever experienced as I baptized Him during His earthly ministry.

Who am I? _____

God Is . . . A GOOD RECORD KEEPER

Day 7

Selah

Our God is good, and He gives us grace and favor as a benefit and reward here on earth. However, never neglect to recognize the reward that is the closeness of His presence when you seek to serve Him with all you have. I encourage you to be intentional in spending time being mindful of this truth today.

_____
_____
_____
_____
_____
_____
_____
_____
_____
_____
_____
_____

Notes

1. Craig Groeschel, *The Christian Atheist: Believing in God but Living As If He Doesn't Exist* (Grand Rapids, MI: Zondervan, 2011).

2. Meister Eckhart, "The Nearness of the Kingdom," Christian Classics Ethereal Library, https://www.ccel.org/ccel/eckhart/sermons.v.html.

3. Jack Wellman, "Top 7 Bible Verses About God's Steadfastness," *Patheos* (blog), Christian Crier, July 26, 2015, https://www.patheos.com/blogs/christiancrier/2015/07/26/top-7-bible-verses-about-gods-steadfastness/.

4. Billy Graham, "Why Easter Matters: 10 Quotes From Billy Graham," Billy Graham Evangelistic Association, April 11, 2019, https://billygraham.org/story/why-easter-matters-10-billy-graham-quotes/.

5. C. S. Lewis, *Mere Christianity* (San Francisco, CA: HarperOne, 2015).

6. Lucado, M. (2007). *Traveling light: Releasing the burdens you were never intended to bear.* Nashville: Thomas Nelson

7. Martin Luther, Christian Quotes, https://www.christianquotes.info/images/martin-luther-quote-gods-hands/.

8. Sylvia Gunter, "God's Sufficiency Exceeds Our Need," Disciplined Spirituality, The Spiritual Life Network, https://www.thespiritlife.net/facets/disciplined/51-paradigm/paradigm-reflection/5098-god-s-sufficiency-exceeds-our-need-by-sylvia-gunter.

9. John Piper, "He Is Like a Refiner's Fire," Desiring God, November 29, 1987, https://www.desiringgod.org/messages/he-is-like-a-refiners-fire.

Quiz Answer Key

Week 1: God Is . . . Always Good!

JOB—Reference Job 1, 2, 3; 13:13–17; 42:10–17

Week 2: God Is . . . Near

THOMAS—Reference John 20:19–29

Week 3: God Is . . . Constant

JOSEPH—Reference Genesis 37, 39–41

Week 4: God Is . . . Love

DAVID – Reference 1 Samuel 16; 2 Samuel 5:1–5; 2 Samuel 11–12

Week 5: God Is . . . My Redeemer

GOMER—Reference Hosea 1, 3

Week 6: God Is . . . My Shepherd

MOSES—Reference Exodus 2:11–14; 3:1–13; 13:17–22; 14; 15:22–27; 16:1–21

Week 7: God Is . . . Peace

PAUL & SILAS—Reference Acts 16:16–34

Week 8: God Is . . . The Well!

THE WIDOW WOMAN—Reference 1 Kings 17

Week 9: God Is . . . A Refiner

THE PRODIGAL SON—Reference Luke 15:11–32

Week 10: God Is . . . A Good Record Keeper

JOHN THE BAPTIST—Reference Matthew 3:1–17

Acknowledgements

Writing a book is harder than I ever imagined and more rewarding than I could have guessed. I am blessed beyond measure with such amazing family, friends, church family and colleagues. I wish I had enough space to thank you all individually, but that would be another book. Just know that I am grateful to each of you for being a part of this journey.

I have to start by thanking the two people that this book is dedicated to: my parents, Pastor Charles & Apostle Ursula White. They exemplified the beauty of living relationally with Christ. Thank you for teaching me the immutability of God's nature regardless of life circumstances.

Thank you to my bonus mom, Tanya! Thank you for staying and for loving and supporting us like your own.

Thank you to my siblings: Vi, Toot, AJ, Ty, and RoRo! Thank you guys for hearing my ideas, telling me when they're dumb, celebrating with me, crying with me, and doing life with me. Y'all *seriously* keep me going.

I must thank my amazing editor, Erin Brown. You went above and beyond to help me navigate the writing for print process and polish my work. (thewriteeditor@gmail.com)

My Pastors and Mentors, Bishop Allen & Pastor Cheryl Rice, have empowered me to do so many things, including this project. Thank you for your prayers and agreement, for your encouragement, support, and impartation.

Finally, I could not have done this without my God Is . . . Squad: Jae, Jakira and Bethany! Thank you ladies a million times for putting up with all of the random texts, my indecisiveness, for your Pinterest boards, hard work, party planning, and suggestions.

Made in the USA
Columbia, SC
18 August 2019